WHAT'S ON MyPlate?

GRAINS on MyPlate

by Mari Schuh

Consulting editor: Gail Saunders-Smith, PhD

Consultant: Barbara J. Rolls, PhD
Guthrie Chair in Nutrition
Pennsylvania State University
University Park, Pennsylvania

CAPSTONE PRESS
a capstone imprint

Pebble Plus is published by Capstone Press,
1710 Roe Crest Drive, North Mankato, Minnesota 56003.
www.capstonepub.com

Library of Congress Cataloging-in-Publication Data
Schuh, Mari C., 1975–
  Grain on MyPlate / by Mari Schuh.
    p. cm.—(Pebble Plus. What's on MyPlate?)
  Includes bibliographical references and index.
  Summary: "Simple text and photos describe USDA's MyPlate tool and healthy grain choices for children"—Provided by publisher.
  ISBN 978-1-4296-8742-3 (library binding)
  ISBN 978-1-4296-9416-2 (paperback)
  ISBN 978-1-62065-327-2 (eBook PDF)
  1. Grain—Juvenile literature.
  SB189.S38 2013
  633.1'7—dc23   2012009312

Editorial Credits
Jeni Wittrock, editor; Sarah Bennett, designer; Svetlana Zhurkin, media researcher; Kathy McColley, production specialist; Sarah Schuette, photo stylist; Marcy Morin, studio scheduler

Photo Credits
All photos by Capstone Studio/Karon Dubke except:
Shutterstock: Aleksandra Duda, cover (top right), Brooke Becker, back cover, Evikka, cover (bottom left), Kaspri, cover (bottom right), Vasyl Dudenko, 7; USDA, cover (inset), 5

The author dedicates this book to her husband, Joseph Quam.

Information in this book supports the U.S. Department of Agriculture's MyPlate food guidance system found at www.choosemyplate.gov. Food amounts listed in this book are based on daily recommendations for children ages 4-8. The amounts listed in this book are appropriate for children who get less than 30 minutes a day of moderate physical activity, beyond normal daily activities. Children who are more physically active may be able to eat more while staying within calorie needs. The U.S. Department of Agriculture (USDA) does not endorse any products, services, or organizations.

Note to Parents and Teachers

The What's on MyPlate? series supports national science standards related to health and nutrition. This book describes and illustrates the USDA's recommendations on the grain food group. The images support early readers in understanding the text. The repetition of words and phrases helps early readers learn new words. This book also introduces early readers to subject-specific vocabulary words, which are defined in the Glossary section. Early readers may need assistance to read some words and to use the Table of Contents, Glossary, Read More, Internet Sites, and Index sections of the book.

Printed in the United States   5547

Table of Contents

MyPlate

Grains are a tasty part of MyPlate. MyPlate is a tool that helps you eat healthful foods.

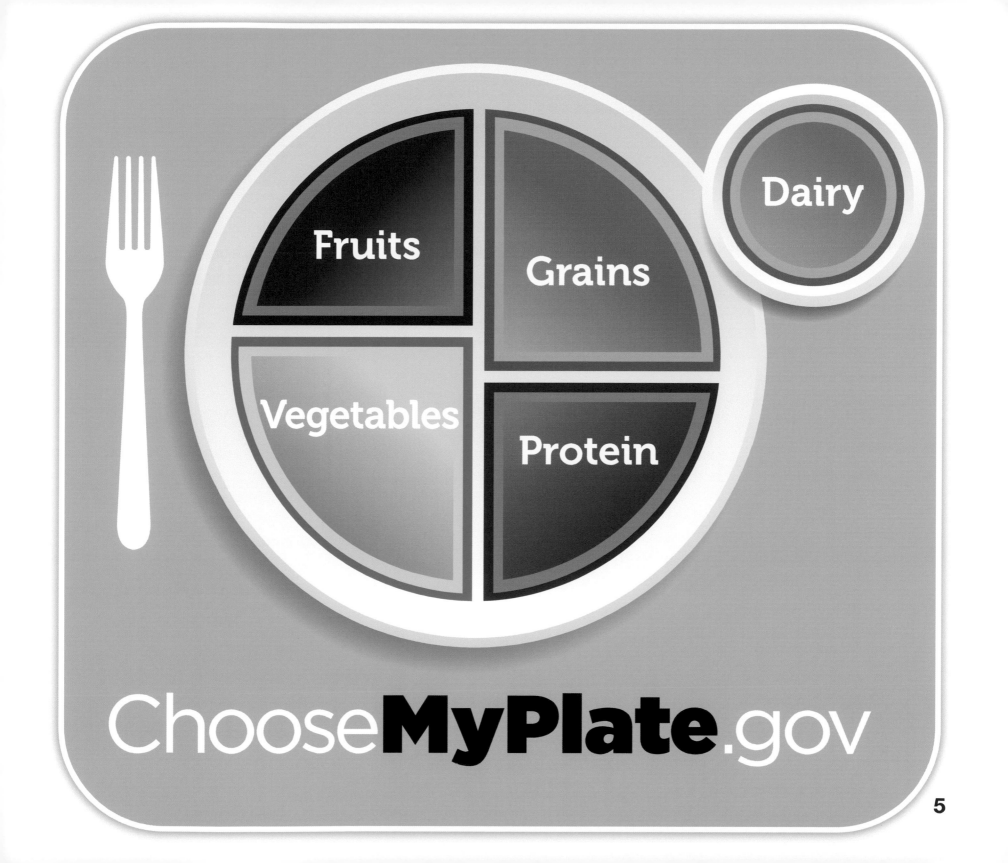

5

Have you seen

grains growing in fields?

Grains are parts of plants.

Wheat, corn, rice,

and oats are grains.

Grains can be whole or refined. Whole grain foods are made from whole kernels of grain. Refined grains are not. Whole grain foods have more nutrients.

refined grains

whole grains

Try to eat 5 ounces (140 grams) of grains every day. Make at least half of your grains whole grains. Check for whole grains on food labels.

Enjoying Grains

Time for breakfast!

Oatmeal is

a quick, warm meal.

Hungry?

Choose a whole grain
bagel with peanut butter
and banana.

Snack time!

Make popcorn

in the microwave.

Share it with your friends.

The noodles in your soup
are made from grain.
Slurp!

Favorite Grains

Grains fill you up
and give you energy.
What are your
favorite grains?

How Much to Eat

Kids need to eat five servings of grain every day. Pick five of your favorite grain foods below. Try to make three of them whole grains.

½ cup (120 mL) cooked whole grain pasta

5 whole wheat crackers

1 slice whole grain bread

½ cup (120 mL) cooked brown rice

½ cup (120 mL) cooked spaghetti

3 cups (720 mL) low fat popcorn

1 mini bagel

1 cup (240 mL) whole grain cereal

Glossary

kernel—a grain or seed of corn, wheat or other cereal plant

MyPlate—a food plan that reminds people to eat healthful food and be active; MyPlate was created by the U.S. Department of Agriculture

nutrient—something that people need to eat to stay healthy and strong; vitamins and minerals are nutrients

refined grain—having only part of a grain seed

serving—one helping of food

whole grain—having all three parts of a grain seed

Read More

Aboff, Marcie. *The Great Grains Group.* MyPlate and Healthy Eating. Mankato, Minn.: Capstone Press, 2012.

Adams, Julia. *Grains.* Good Food. New York: PowerKids Press, 2011.

Tourville, Amanda Doering. *Fuel the Body: Eating Well.* How to Be Healthy! Minneapolis: Picture Window Books, 2009.

Internet Sites

FactHound offers a safe, fun way to find Internet sites related to this book. All of the sites on FactHound have been researched by our staff.

Here's all you do:

Visit *www.facthound.com*

Type in this code: 9781429687423

 Check out projects, games and lots more at **www.capstonekids.com**

Index

Word Count: 143
Grade: 1
Early-Intervention Level: 16